Beneath

Also by Simon Perril

Poetry
Archilochus on the Moon
Newton's Splinter
Nitrate
A Clutch of Odes
Hearing is Itself Suddenly a Kind of Singing

Criticism
The Salt Companion to John James
Tending the Vortex: the Works of Brian Catling

Simon Perril

Beneath
—*A Nekyiad*

Shearsman Books

First published in the United Kingdom in 2015 by
Shearsman Books
50 Westons Hill Drive
Emersons Green
BRISTOL
BS16 7DF

Shearsman Books Ltd Registered Office
30–31 St. James Place, Mangotsfield, Bristol BS16 9JB
(this address not for correspondence)

www.shearsman.com

ISBN 978-1-84861-440-6

Copyright © Simon Perril, 2015.

The right of Simon Perril to be identified as the author
of this work has been asserted by him in accordance with the
Copyrights, Designs and Patents Act of 1988.
All rights reserved.

ACKNOWLEDGEMENTS
Some of these poems have appeared in *Cordite Review*.
My thanks to the editors for their interest and support.

*This one is for Elly,
who came from nowhere,
and changed everything:
thank you!*

1.

who will hold
a black ram's head
flush to the ground
over the rough cup
of a trench

open a second mouth
in its neck
to drool its red life through

and command me
drink, spout truth you
who were more shade above
in the mud-brick groves
of kitchens

than here beneath
where I run no errand
save to find

a utensil
shaped like a mouth
strung like a loom
to sing through

2.

Hermes took me down
each step
I left a deposit

Hermes took me down
each step
decreased in sound

Hermes took me down
each step
the ground forgave

Hermes took me down
each step
the flowers looked away

Hermes took me down
each step
beneath the grave

Hermes took me down
each step
a ghost note

Hermes took me down
each step I regret
he left me

3.

I do not recall
arrival
at Acheron

Charon having taken
express delivery:

one pale jar
neck stopped

4.

that first night
adrift

Lethe dyed my thoughts
white

and I wore them
anew, so fresh

they barely contained
you

5.

Father, once I saw
you throw a stone
atop a cairn

leaving the weight
in your limbs there
on that pile

I smile now
each of my arms
and legs crammed

with wet black sand;
know I carry you
my trunk

a chest of oak
washed up
on this dark shore

6.

hold your ears
stop them

for when nothing
comes in

these holes
so difficult to close

you hold
what shades hold

7.

in Hades
the one sound property

is to recall
your bodily monody

blood-thump
bone-creak

murmurs
of distant springs

8.

my sister went first
we'd a pact

that after crossing
she'd show she'd left

by gripping a weft
of unspooled wool

white-nuckle tight.
In the event she swung

and I saw the slug
of her tongue

and wept
at her outstretched palm

9.

I dreamt I bathed
at dusk
in the leathered sea

and close by me
a bee
perched on a wave-scale

I tipped it
– not from spite,
 so's I might

darken those stripes:
wet bands
bobbed in my hand

10.

these hands
have dipped in the lip-mauve pocket
of slit fish

these hands
have scooped the wet gut-gems
inside

these hands
have peeled bone-fans
apart

these hands
have primed white meat
in lemon and thyme

these hands
have baked the white flakes
of flesh

what hands
performed such rites on me
so far from the sea?

11.

nightfall's quick-step
on the never-to-be-blue
hue of dawn

has torn the lining
right out
– no embers in the sky

rosy-fingers withdrawn
yet I
have somehow kept

the promise of colour
young skin holds
awaiting touch

12.

my thoughts reverse
about-turn of a shoal
labouring
at a temporary mirror

like the backward flow
of water here
under green sun
in soil skies

walk past the silvered cypress
past the black bubbling
vase of the Styx
we are arranged in

no sound from the half-waked
bells of Asphodel
as I range the meadow
waist deep

seeking Mnemosyne's cup
to sup my thoughts
right-side up

13.

my mouth rusts
with obule dust
fat tongue

– no shapen oar –
can't paddle
this shallow cave

no scene of rites
no dim-lit nights
no offerings

at the edge
of these stone lips
no sound within the tunnel

14.

these pores that lace
this thing I move
around in, breathe
in the dank

I am
a chorus of gasps
no lyre can pluck

15.

all turn
to Hades
House of the Unseen

discontinued
democracy of the dead
in total recess

the only toil here
contemplation
of soil

the poverty of shadows
the property of Pluto
god of used goods

16.

I keep a map
of the sleep I sweep
to the corners,
margins of my kitchens

for all the specks
collected from floors above
have gathered
in my dark office below

and I know from Father
a map is what you slap
over another land
you want to take

here I cook nothing
but a dark soup
grave-deep
and heavily seasoned

17.

the confusion
of flower-beds
at dusk

is mine
alternating hues
I transport them

pieces of sky
gathered by my eye
from above

I lay on the ground
below
carpeting Persephone's bedroom

18.

in the classroom
of the dead

I learn netherspeak
a breach

between thought
and tongue

I come to cross
in my pale craft

for home is housed
not by the dead

but the inner labyrinths
of the dreaming head

19.

blossoms lodge
in my throat

who spilt flowers here
planted saplings?

I croak coming spring
in the dark

there is no green
yet my skin

gathers dew
in the black morning

20.

grass-pale
I'm a silver thread
blown through the undergroves

sing iced wind
through the apple-boughs
faster, faster

and I'll knit all this
shuttle my song
among the trees

my crooked loom

21.

I seek song
among the shades
of black

I seek song
among the lack
of green

from the pink
ribs of my cave mouth
I keen

trying notes
these
sound mysteries

22.

my love, you've seen
the underside
of a swan's wing;

know I've never been
so white as here
my fan of bones

never so strong
as when I walk
the dark groves

who knows
it's not wet grass trod to milk
under my feet

23.

I drink the *kybeon*
cool and long
as Demeter supped it

searching
with moth tenacity
for Persephone

yet she has a garden
and I
have fallen below

the soil;
aspire to push
up dust.

My head breaks
the surface
these dry waves

24.

no goose-skein
rains arrows across mottled-skies

here,
only night's bruise

a heart hanging
ripe in my chest

I fear to shake

25.

soldier dear
Father offered you
my hand
then withdrew it
– my cheeks fired terracotta –

then I withdrew
a stool
and all Thasos
magistrates and men of state
took my hand
– fired grey-blue –

clean off;
buried it apart
in a separate bed
fearing its next move

26.

in Hades' household
the walls bloom
Lethe green

I have been
picked
for this dark vase

27.

I overheard Father tell
how thrice Odysseus
stretched for Anticleia
to reach right through her
in shadow-dance
the moves
curled dye in water

then wives and daughters
followed, flocked
to the bloody trench
a throng of wrong.

Father, soldier, lover
to whom do I belong?
Never mother,
now I nurse
a gift for dispersal

join the gloom
so industriously turned
on Persephone's loom
by the ebony throne

28.

no thorn-crowned boy
served bread from a sieve
in the house of my Father

I remain
a Melian vessel
peer

through these holes
see in the dark
the workings above;

veil a woman
wall a city
cork a bottle

the treachery
of the sea
means nothing to me

29.

on Thasos
I lost my face,
if ever it was
my place to own one.

In the House of the Dead,
I lost my head,
Persephone buried it
In the hearth-black earth.

In Hades
I misplaced the rest,
it spilt as from
an alabastron;
how far the mind runs

to a squall now
never straight
no body to navigate

30.

in the house of the death god
I wash and wish
the dish of lake Acheron
would serve my face

in the house of the death god
I wash and wish
I was more than white barley meal
strewn on water

in the house of the death god
I wash and wish
to alter this daughter's cloth
fill it with shape and weight

in the house of the death god
I wash and wish
this ache
had a home of flesh and bone

in the house of the death god
I wash and wish
dread Persephone would walk back with me
up to the light

in the house of the death god
I wash and wish
the grey of the mead
was upon my hair

as if I'd worn it there
so long
in the salt air
of the Aegean

31.

my thoughts
are thieves
take flesh I've lost

lust
after shapes
I've been

so open
I am emptied
note

nagging
in the throat
of a flute

blown
clean
away

32.

that water
such skin!

and I'm
so lacking

the low pines
shed needles

33.

netherspeak
reaches beneath, burrows

below tonsil's counsel
deep under all lids

nine anvils deep
where, Father told me

Zeus keeps
his darkest tricks

Tantalus
of perpetual reach

up at low-hung fruit
down to pool

he drools for;
all retreats

as skin from bone
all the wrangle and wrong

in nightside song
speaks this:

gone to Tartarus' pit
darker

than Zeus' eye socket

34.

you enter
my dark office
under heavy shadows

that fall
under everyday things
that refuse to sing
being so cruelly worked

I entered later
than the kindness I once saw
shown to the bones of a nag
in lightening the load
on its back

I entered of a sudden
kick of a stool
wronged by a song

35.

soldier dear,
here is where I,
dust mote
on Stygian puddle,
settle

not certain scores
nor heroic annals
that dry on the skins
– they won't name us women:

here says Neobulé,
a trembling in the grass
at night, dapple on water
under moonlight;

the concealed sound
of kitchenware
in search of cupboard.

Archilochus, I flicked
the milk-scab gift
your staff wept
on my limbs

and underneath
there is a white
of no colour

36.

in Persephone's precinct
I am traversed, twitch
like a dog in dream

hear only
my hiss and hum

in Persephone's precinct
I am reversed, patch
the black by blinking shards of blue

hear only
my hiss and hum

in Persephone's precinct
I converse, stitch
myself back to front

hear only
my hiss and hum

in Persephone's precinct
I nurse, name
the contours of kitchens

hear only
my hiss and hum

in Persephone's precinct
I remain, knead
my shame

here only
I hiss and hum
an inner maelstrom

37.

away Neobulé, you are
a way, passage
soft water makes

as it breaks through the pores
of the earth
sweats a cave beneath

hood for poor shades
to pause under
gathering wefts

they shuttle
with no anticipation
of cloth to come

38.

grave shades, you
who have had your fill
emptied

are spilt
decanted
in frantic wisps

chill as cave-air
wet as breath
death is

life's undercoat:
wear it
out

39.

all know
of the cricket's friction
but few tell
how Aphrodite's sole
rarely rests
on the tortoise shell

but gently shuttles
'cross its ridges
back and forth
but not for warmth

40.

fear the tortoise, girls
– not its shell

but the single scale
of its head

41.

Archilochus, no Orpheus
will come for me

wife-to-be
hung up and cut down

sent off-scene, dropped
through earth-exit

neck
pomegranate red

stripe
on my white sheet

shade
of that third share

bang your head
beneath

on the cold ground
in grave counsel

42.

Demeter did it,
planted the bulbs of my eyes
in the undersoil

drained those dark points
that brim in shallow pockets
closest the nose-bridge

pools that seep
leak beetle-black
legs that run from me

carrying my shell

43.

when lunar light
greases night's cloth
I've an urge

to wipe it to a smear,
secrete my signature
where material's thinnest.

I need no point,
can peak without pricking
where the lining's wettest

44.

Dionysus
god in the tree

whose limbs of ivy
curled 'cross Thracian seas

will come for me
and plant a wet kiss

reclaim his daughter
as a body

of dancing water

45.

at Hades' marketplace
an assembly of shades
– their stuttering accounts
amount to nothing

I crave the rave-god
man-tearer
dance-dealer

neglected shuttle and loom
when the room leaked
milk and wine
kissed the vine-stiff Thyrsos

felt the flame
on my upturned throat
the nick and tug
of the kid at my breast

smelt pine-torch
and the musk
of my fawn skin

its dappled tufts
o god nurse
my wet elements

46.

I have been to sea
so rarely
and understand its depths
– they don't concern me

yet amongst the trees
that stand heavy
beside the weighty wheels
of Hades' chariot

what impresses me
is the mystery of anchors,
how even flowers
have plinths of green

47.

Archilochus,
what Maenad hands
dealt to many a bull
I bequeathe to you:

may your hooves
and offal
coat the pine-fir
and drip there
for my pleasure.

Even in Hades
the god in my white
translucent fingers
still lingers

48.

they never buried me
with the loutrophoros
for company

that carrier of wedding waters
blessed
with elongated neck

for mine was thick enough,
taut from the tug
of wrong,
densely woven,
song

49.

I knew a foreign god
who trod all drudge to wine

a foreign god
who scattered wits

like olive pits
spat at mud

a foreign god
who ushered in

the othering trance
with a tap from his fennel-lance

pushed mind to dance
sheer into nonsense

the foreign god
to whom I'd climb

up thick green vines
out of here

50.

as a girl I wrapped my pet
and buried it
a muddle of wings
and jellied things.

There was no door
in the floor of the earth
though I knocked.

That life stalks death
in such short steps
I did not expect

51.

I was ready to disappear,
leave my Father's house;
to arrive someone else
though I never thought
who that would be.

I was ready to disappear,
vacate my Father's house
as a soft mouse does by dawn
through a hole
in the kitchen floor.

I was ready to disappear,
escape my Father's house
as dust does
forced under a door.

I was ready to disappear,
slip from my Father's house
as pine needles
flee their tree.

I was ready to disappear,
seep from my Father's house,
breath above a bowl
of hot broth

I was not ready to appear,
here, deep underneath;
an untoasted gift

dropped
through the box of the ground
in a country
that carries no sound.

52.

I may have been a nurse,
knelt in furs,
at the foot of something
other than a loom

yet I was soon weaving,
spinning immaterial,
a leaving of limbs
on the edge of mountains

where we'd be trees
with trunks of saffron
dancing away from home

53.

I am so far out of doors
further than I was
on many nights
roofless on the rocks
under silver trees

I am so far out of doors
further than I was
when the fennel-wand
leaked honey
and I courted no husband
but a fawnskin god
whose ivy locks
had coiled 'cross ocean floors
to announce the dance

I am so far out of doors
further than I was
when wrapped
in snake-skin girdle
my reason curdled
and I was whey

I am so far out of doors
yet think of Him
sewn into the skin
of Zeus's thigh
and dream
how we beat time
to a trance

54.

when Eros licked me alight
I was open
let the wind play
in the gateway
of my mouth

when Eros licked me alight
it was night
in my belly
and a steady stream
ran in the cave below

when Eros licked me alight
I was a blister
I'd seen on the palm
of my sister
keenly worked

when Eros licked me alight
I lay like water
stirred
into rings
by dropped things

when Eros licked me alight
I broke my banks
fled
into the hyacinth beds
bent them flat

when Eros licked me alight
I lost all shape
and weight
and no nuptial cape
could hold or hide me

55.

the last part of me
to lose the art of weight
was the tongue

as above
none would hear it
for long

it belongs below
in the dark dumbshow
of the damned

56.

when, under your stool,
your foot falls
to sleep
no longer carries you

shortly, there is a fizzing
like the pulse of a spring;
I would give anything
for that ache,
that returning

to be a bulb
have shape
possess weight
that might shoot

57.

I am perplexed
to be left
in the dark grass
holding the heavy sieve
of the Danaidai

those wilful girls,
daughters in slaughter,
passed it for safekeep
yet both my hands shake
with the gift

and I half suspect the gait
of a market inspector
to judge my weight unfair

for this swap is so:
I have leaked away
like a stray stream
In the dog days

and steam is all
that remains;
a slight stain
on the kitchen ceiling
amongst the other shades

58.

let he
who has no taste
for rind
not find the moist heart
of an artichoke.

Let she
who keeps loose her hair
and still has use
of her toys
– tambourine and ball –
make joyous noise:

all that remains
is that itch
in that other mouth
none have reached

59.

Archilochus, how
has my heart
gained weight

on this diet
save with greedy glances
at the lard moon

– you've seen the chunks I've taken
now rest in them:
my holes

60.

my skin
has never been
so direct a map

as that would level peaks
lay cool pathways
to the sea.

I pool resources
would shame Pluto.

Damn in cunning iambs
all you like
you'll not dam me:

I sluice

61.

when you tread above me
it snows soil,
flecks of your weary steps
I carry in my curls

when you pace above me
your footfall lands
in the fluttering skin
at the outskirts of my palms

when you pound above me
with the force of a sea,
Archilochus dear,
I am happy to be here:

a wraith who never felt
your clammy weight
heave upon me

62.

the dead
have no head for sleep
yet I dreamt in dark groves

how you drenched my brow
with bee-balm;
and I sprouted extremities
clutched
through these utensils for touch

– yet these limbs
belonged to nothing;
I am tomorrow's bread
unlevened, flat
and yet to set

63.

my knees
carry less of me
where I kneel

they are not
so scaled, etched
with patterned floors

no maps
no nets
delimit my surfaces

I run or stand
a body
of water

persist
untouched in zones
between ankle and wrist

64.

on the shore
the Fates sit, unpick
that which I was
stitch by stitch

I am dropped
like the night sky above
laid flat below
spread like a dark veil

before the Styx
whose depths
don't turn or run
for they are thicker than honey

glazed like the black terracotta
a daughter prizes
as the shape of a baby's bottle

yet I am weaned here
off weight and gait
let loose
from all vestiges of shape

65.

green dill shoots
from the mouth
of the red mullet

he of the bright stripe
and double beard
that bottom-feeding fish

buried in mud
whose blood-belly
and brilliant scales

progressively fail
in the closing tale
towards table.

In his vacant gawp
and clouded gaze
I am dissembled:

the slow fall
of a loose shawl
about my ankles

66.

what's to relay
of the bubble-pout
of my other mouth

now I've no finger
for it to grip
yet I'm landed

a splash
on the dark shore

67.

at night
in the half-light
honeycomb flicker
of kitchen clutter

I have seen
the skin on the milk-jug
tremble

68.

on the forest floor
the more you look

those feathers
like you change

from black
through blue

to a hole in colour
you crawl through

reach beneath
that vacuum

between mouth
and teeth

69.

in the heart of the wood
I could see nothing
so clearly I could touch it

brush against its tunic
and clasp it
as my own.

Eight legs of night
climb my spine
wing each shoulder

if I am so much colder now
what of that melt
around my middle

of that spittle-core
you once saw,
soldier dear,

in a wood unlike this
and could not seal
even with a kiss.

How that mouth chatters here
through the gaps in the branches
through the lapse I am

whistling
llke a goatherd
conjuring flock

70.

I recall
in all this under-muddle
that breath
that swayed the curtains
at dawn

as the room exhaled
my skin
welcomed it in

that light tremor
across all surfaces
as day begins

and something
under the skin
sings

71.

Father bored me with lessons
on botany and plant lore, properties

of saps, roots, leaves
buds, flowers, fruits

for then I held my own flush
fresh upon me

brighter than the Butcher's Broom
a bloom of coral-red berries

strewn 'cross my breast
– though you never lay flush against me

I tended my flora
sustained with plentiful moisture

paddled in my own pool
alone

72.

only once did Father's lesson stick
and I feel its worth
here under the earth:

he spoke with awe
of the tulip deep
in its dust-bed

how it wears wool
between outer skin
and inner core

of the finest fleece,
the envy of Arachne.
With such artistry

it webs a cloak fine yet thick
and this slick garment
keeps it moist

73.

Aspidion,
translucent shield

curious capsule
that holds light when seeds are gone

tell me, what
is the plot

in the fleshy folds
of this buried bulb?

Not even the milk
a poppy head weeps

may grant me sleep

74.

Father, I recall a leaning wall
of logs, bark removed,
skin smooth

aslant around a pole
placed at the centre
of the pile

with careful attention
given to the space
between the stacks;

for that is where the draught
comes, through this opening
and when all

is covered with earth
and lit with straw and twigs
through a hole in the top

these gaps suck
flames lick
leave us charcoal tips

to line our kilns
fire our shapes
smelt our coin

and a drip of tar and pitch
to paint on boat ribs
to aid their journey.

But why,
in these ashlands
marched by the silent bells

and corpse-like smells of asphodels,
this memory
so clear and dear to me

if not for its testimony
to my incomplete
and ribless destiny

as smoke's trip
from white to blue
to empty into air

75.

this House
of Hades

accommodates all us women
swept to its great halls;

we are this matter of dirt
untraced in the dark

repose
for fallen shadows.

Its great depths
are not an ocean's chest

they are much closer
to the hearth

the flickering aftermath
of kitchens

the migrant's deep dream
of home

76.

Father kissed me
towards the end

and I thought then
of all the other things
that stop

77.

Persephone, dark abductee
gather me

for I soften
lose shape

find kin
amongst the wet things

palpitate
like a fountain tip.

So slit the pocket
of my back

reach in
unfold the flutes there

make me
a set of wings

so I might
leave

78.

hold me
up to the light

you'll find
the perforated underside

of the myrtle.
Water leaves, is

constant leaving
a leaking

from holes, cracks
in dry lands

folds of face
and lower creases.

Relish this race
to the edges:

banish all thought
that it ceases

79.

no boats, none
graze the surface
of this lake

yet I take
off this skirt
hoist sail;

o little craft
go elsewhere
for dawn's

fit to break

80.

what holds me
when even the mystery
of the smallest bones in the body
has gone

those spindle sticks
cast no shade
on my inmost shape
and I pass between:

no bride
no mother
no queen

the dwindling prospect
of a lover
in the leaving light

Netherspeak: an afterward(s)

I had never intended to stay so long in the clutches of ancient lyric, but its grasp proved formidable. It has allowed me to continue to explore aspects of poetry that have long intrigued me: just how does a poem hold, and with what kind of grip? I have long favoured the poetic sequence, prompted by an early encounter with Spicer's serial poem, for its porous qualities. Its interstices permit the passage of ideas and sounds across and between poems, as if liquid was being passed through a series of inadequate hands. Does the lyric body possess a particular physiology? Anne Carson, ruminating upon a fragment of Archilochus, suggests the primacy of the lungs. The fragment has Eros coiled beneath the lover's heart "filching out of my chest the soft lungs". Carson quips "naturally, this ends the poem: with the organ of breath gone, speech is impossible". But she also explores these lyric lungs – the *phrenes* – for their connection to expanded notions of breath inseparable from perception and emotion in ancient Greek thought: "words, thoughts, and understanding are both received and produced by the *phrenes*. So words are 'winged' in Homer when they issue from the speaker and 'unwinged' when they are kept in the *phrenes* unspoken. *Phrenes* are organs of mind."

Peter Green's *Shadow of the Parthenon* suggests "Neobulé's side of the story would be worth hearing – like Molly Bloom's". The suggestion was logged, somehow, somewhere, only to emerge with more urgency on a car journey to Nottingham. I was on my way, excitedly, to an exhibition of the drawings of the artist and writer Alfred Kubin. Kubin's late Symbolist work is phantastical and otherworldly, full of decadent morbidity and eroticism executed in a luminous, opulent pen and ink that belies the description black and white. Whilst driving, the image that gave me Neobulé's circumstances was thinking about *The Swamp*, reproduced in the pre-exhibition pamphlet. Only when I came to write this afterward did I realise – tumbling through my vinyl – the potency of this image had built since teenage years when I had bought an obscure album, *Music from the Ante Chamber*, by Robert Haigh, with a very poor and unattributed reproduction of the Kubin image on the cover. In the small pamphlet reproduction a naked woman tentatively enters a pool, her pose conveying the awkwardness of maintaining balance; perhaps it is the temperature of the liquid that threatens this, perhaps it is the instability of the bottom that would swallow her. Only when your gaze averts from her plight do you notice the shadows above her are the visages – seemingly in conversation – of three amphibious deities overlooking the scene. I then realised that my *Archilochus on the Moon* was unfinished business; his exiled bid to colonise the moon, with all its bitter bravado, had a twin. What of Neobulé, betrothed to the soldier poet only to have their marriage cancelled, forced by her father's sense of family shame in the wake of iambic slurs to take her own life? In the composition of Kubin's image I saw her as a newly arrived shade, dipping her limbs into the waters of the underworld. In the texture of Kubin's image – the exhibition notes nod to "an innovative airspray technique, which emulates the tonal effects of aquatint in etching and looks almost photographic by the standards of the day" – I had my challenge. The first couple of poems I wrote were just wrong – and too *wronged*. I didn't want her to be relegated to Archilochus' ironic bluster, his virtuoso volatility. In Kubin's ambient brushwork – wash and spray on paper were distinct hallmarks of his practice – I had a model for a lightness of voice. I wanted poems that would barely graze the page, as Neobulé gradually comes to terms with her insubstantiality, her shade-hood. In the afterward to *Archilochus on the Moon* I spoke of lyric vestments and a sense of voice as garment. The voice of the sixth-century soldier-poet was brash, uneven – sticky from friction. Neobulé's needed to be increasingly deliquescent, porous; the "netherspeak" of shadehood mourning substance.

In *Eros the Bittersweet*, Anne Carson explains that "Eros is an issue of boundaries … the interval between reach and grasp". Neobulé's underworld journey traces the trajectory of eros that "moves out from the lover toward the beloved, then ricochets back to the lover himself and the hole in him, unnoticed before." But in this instance the lover *herself* notices. Carson asks "who is the real subject of most love poems? Not the beloved. It is that hole". In the halls and meadows of Hades, Neobulé feels a desire racing through her that she can no longer house. If she frequently reaches for repetition it is an attempt to gather herself in sound.

Erin Mouré's remarkable excursion into Mediaeval Galician Cantigas, in *O Cadoiro*, has been a constant companion in my own journey into the tangled roots of lyric. She writes of encountering the materiality of these songbooks where – even in a lithographical reproduction of a photographic facsimile of the sixteenth-century manuscript, itself a copy – 'writing itself scratches the lyric' in script that makes palpable a propelled, secular, yearning. She writes of how 'sonority breaks against the readers' own langue de fond as surprise and murmur'; and I knew I wanted to cultivate this undulation of desire devoid of later, Dantescan, prospects of salvation and new life. Neobulé's underworld needed an emotional geography, and I found it in the concrete environments of the Cantigas, with their seas, ships, flowers, cobbles and the washing of lovers' shirts worn closest to the skin.

References to Neobulé within the corpus of Archilochus fragments are sparse. She is there by metonymy; a clutch of limbs. And, despite the potency of the myth of the Lycambids' fate, many scholars argue for the typological function of the 'real names' scattered throughout the poems. The fact that Neobulé means "she who makes new plans" resonates beyond the tale of her doomed marriage. In the mid-'70s the papier-mâché wrappings of a mummy in Vienna disclosed the fullest fragment yet of an Archilochus poem; and one that differs from the existing corpus in what it brings to Neobulé's situation. Commonly known as the *Cologne Epode*, this new papyrus contained 35 lines from the middle and end of a poem in which the poet tells of an amorous encounter with a young woman. His sexual advances are blocked. Not by Neobulé, but by her younger sister. When this sister evokes marriage and suggests he turn his attentions back to her older sibling, it provokes an outburst about how Neobulé is "overripe, her girlhood bloom has withered"; she has "never yet kept down her lust", and is "faithless" and "two-faced". Guy Davenport places this in the context of the ritual cursing Archilochus is famous for. But this damning of Neobulé's sexuality contains familiar gender politics.

A later Anne Carson essay attends to Ancient Greek society's focus upon *miasmata*; codes of "defilements" that helped govern the threat posed by female pollution. She explores how "physiologically, women are wet", the opposite of "dry" mental stability and alertness. She notes that "The emotions of Eros are especially liquid and liquefying. Eros pours, drips, heats, softens, melts, loosens, cools, boils, dissolves." Greek marriage is the means through which men control the wildness of Eros, and yet women in Greek thought are not merely associated with boundaries that patrol the perimeter of order; they are also interiors removed from the centre of culture and politics. It is an interiority that Zeitlin suggests is "spatialized as an underworld", with Persephone's descent an "equivalent to the initiation of the female into her own interior space". My Neobulé is beneath; and whilst she navigates both the underworld and her slow-dawning dissolution, she recalls the shadehood of women's life above. The tender ambivalence she feels to her soldier-suitor is tempered by her knowledge of Dionysus, the "foreign god" of cultic ecstasy. If she were "more shade above / in the mud-brick groves / of kitchens", then such rituals provide alternatives, however temporary, to the limitations of the domestic sphere. Zeitlin notes such occasions were "probably the only legitimate reasons for leaving the house" but adds that "the attraction of women for his cult represents both a symptom which drives them from their homes and a cure which sends them back again."

FURTHER READING FOR THE CURIOUS
Anne Carson, *Eros the Bittersweet*
Anne Carson, 'Putting her in her place: Woman, Dirt and Desire' in David M. Halperin, John J. Winkler, Froma I Zeitlin, eds. *Before Sexuality: The Construction of Erotic Experience in the Ancient Greek World.*

Guy Davenport, 'Archilochus "Epode: Fireworks on the Grass"', *The Hudson Review*, vol 28, No.3 (Autumn, 1975) pp. 352-356

Peter Green, *The Shadow of the Parthenon: Studies in Ancient History and Literature.*

H.D. Rankin, 'The New Archilochus and Some Archilochean Questions', *Quaderni Urbinati di Cultura Classica*, No. 28 (1978) pp. 7-27

Froma I. Zeitlin, 'Cultic models of the Female: Rites of Dionysus and Demeter', *Arethusa 15*, no.1 and 2, (Spring and Fall 1982) pp. 129-157